WALK
Going The Distance!

by Ultra-Distance Race-Walker
Richard McChesney

WALK
Going The Distance!

First edition published 2015 by Strictly Business Limited

STRICTLY
BUSINESS

ISBN 978-1-909943-08-7

DEDICATION

To my wife, Ruth. Thanks for all the support you have given me since I started running again in 2006, and race-walking in 2012. Thanks for putting up with the alarm going off in the early hours of a Saturday or Sunday morning so that I could get out for a walk before even the birds wake up.

Thanks for collecting me from races and training walks which finished miles from where they started, for having dinner ready when I got home from after-work training walks, and for being my biggest supporter.

Also thanks to those people who have supported me during the races I have competed in during 2015 - especially Zac, Jim, Jamie, Sarah, and also Suzanne and the many other athletes that I have raced with. Without your support on race day, I would not have achieved the distances and times that I did.

CONTENTS

CHAPTER 1
INTRODUCTION

This book is a consolidation of the race reports I have written from my five major races in 2015 - all between 100 and 176 miles in distance - as well as my thoughts on my training throughout the year.

After my last race, I needed to give my body and mind some time to recover so it seemed an ideal time to write this book before I embarked on my training for 2016. It has being a kind of debrief after a long hard year as well as an opportunity to reminisce - remembering both the highlights (such as walking from Birmingham to London down the Grand Union Canal and walking laps of a 1,000 metre circuit in France for three consecutive days) and the hardships (it isn't easy walking 100 miles or further non-stop).

I also wanted to write this to show you what you can achieve. I haven't really done anything special. I have simply gone for some very long walks – and then written and reflected about them. Hopefully some of the people that read this might be inspired to chase their own goals.

And I am hoping that I might sell a few copies of this book to help fund next year's races. But more about that later.

I am a 47 year old New Zealander living in London. I was previously a reasonably good runner, but always struggled with injuries, so in 2012 I took up race-walking after being frustrated by an on-going impact related ankle injury. I couldn't run at all without pain, but it didn't hurt when I walked.

I had seen some race-walking on TV when watching the Olympics and the Commonwealth Games. It looked so un-natural and was never something I considered doing until I met a Andrew Shelley – the current (at the time) NZ 100km record holder – who walked a 60km race that I was running. I was amazed by the fact that he could walk so far, and so fast. Talking to Andrew later on I discovered that there is a difference between elite race-walking and ultra-distance race-walking. With elite race-walking the walker has to maintain a straight leg from the time the leading foot hits the ground until the hips move over the top of the knee (i.e. the leading leg must be straight at all times) and one foot must be touching the ground at all times. For distances longer than 50km (the longest distance they race in the Olympics), and for any shorter races that are judged under 'B' grade rules, the only rule is that one foot must be touching the ground at all times.

Anyway, 19 months later, in August 2011, I was struggling with an injury again. I was in the middle of a two hour run around Richmond Park (one of my favourite running routes) and my knee was so painful that I stopped running and power-walked home. This lead me to a few more training walks and then I walked a marathon in September followed by another one in December.

When my injury settled I stopped walking and started running again, completing four marathons over the next few months before sustaining another injury.

I was beginning to think that maybe this race-walking lark was for me. I decided to give it a go and I entered my fifth marathon of 2012 as a walker. I managed to finish third in 5 hours and 13 minutes. Two months later I improved my PB (personal best) to 4:53. I tried to combine being both a runner and a race-walker for the next few months but after completing the London marathon in 2013 I gave up running in favour of walking.

I completed my first 100 mile walking race in October 2013 and another in August 2014. I followed that up with 115 miles in 28 hours in Roubaix the following month and from there my story continues …

CHAPTER 2
WINTER TRAINING

My goal over the winter of 2014/15 was to build a solid base of mileage culminating with a 24 hour race in Bourges, France at the end of February. I took a few weeks break, following my 28 hour race in Roubaix , and then I slowly resumed my training and built up my weekly mileage. The days got shorter and shorter so the majority of my training was at night. I found myself spending many hours wandering the streets of South West London between the hours of 8pm and midnight.

On the Saturday night before Christmas, while others were out enjoying pre-Christmas festivities Suzanne Beardsmore, a training and racing partner, and I spent a night walking up and down the road that runs through Bushy Park in Teddington. It is exactly one mile between the two gates of the park and our plan was to walk 50 miles while the park was closed to traffic. The gates are closed from 7pm until 6am during the winter months (and during the hours of darkness in summer) making the flat stretch of road perfect for race-walking. I covered the 50 miles in 10 hours and 32 minutes which was pleasing given that it was dark and I always walk slower in darkness. The real goal of the night was to train myself to walk through the night without struggling to stay awake. I had desperately wanted to sleep in all three of my previous 100 mile races and figured that the best way to get used to walking through the night was to have a normal day and then set off for my walk after dinner.

It was a nice calm evening and while Suzanne and I walked at different speeds, it was fun to share the park with someone through the night. We would pass each other as we walked in opposite directions every 12 to 13 minutes and occasionally we would walk together for a little bit. Suzanne called it a night after about 40 miles as she had a club race the following afternoon, but we both benefited significantly from our first long walks since competing at Roubaix.

January 2015 was to be my big training month with a walk of six hours or longer every weekend and one weekend of back to back 6 hour walks (Saturday and Sunday). I also took the opportunity to travel to different parts of London each Saturday morning and would either run or walk a 5km parkrun (see www.parkrun.com) at 9am and then go for a wander and explore the area. Sometimes I would walk to parkrun, complete the 5km, and then walk back home. Other times I would explore the local area for a few hours and then use Google Maps on my cell phone to find my way back to my car.

At the end of January Suzanne and I completed another Bushy Park overnight 50 miler. This time it was so cold that the water in our bottles had a layer of ice on top. But it was dead calm and I managed to complete my 50 miles in a quicker time of 10 hours and 22 minutes. We were joined in the middle of the night by another race-walker, Sue Clements, who made the trip down from Cambridge to walk with us for 20 miles, and as with the December Bushy Park overnighter, it was a great evening and a real confidence builder to get in a solid 50 mile training walk.

Unfortunately a week after that walk I started to feel unwell after completing an early morning long walk and a parkrun and ended up in bed for a week with a lung infection (caused by too many nights out walking and inhaling too much cold air). I had a further two weeks of no training which put paid to any plans for a 24 hour race at the end of February. Fortunately I was able to get back into training during the last two weeks of February and by mid-March I was fully recovered and ready to start tapering for my first race of the year.

CHAPTER 3
CHATEAU-THIERRY 24 HOUR RACE

The 36th Chateau-Thierry 24 hour race-walking event was held on the 28th and 29th of March 2015. For me, this was going to be a big event. My first race in six months and, with plenty of training miles in the bank, I felt that I could achieve my goal of going under 21 hours for 100 miles and completing a total distance of 115 miles (both of which would beat the current New Zealand records).

The weekend started off when Zac (my 14 year old son and support crew) and I collected Suzanne Beardsmore from the Richmond railway station for the drive down to Dover to catch the ferry to France. The drive to Dover was 108 miles. My current PB for 24 hours was 107 miles. Was this a good omen - that a PB was on the cards?

The trip to Chateau-Thierry was uneventful, consisting of driving a total of 330 miles with a ferry trip in the middle. I have a clear memory of a group of motorcyclists on the ferry wearing Hells Angels jackets and we wondered whether their planned weekend's activities would be harder on the body than ours.

We didn't arrive in Chateau-Thierry until early evening and we went straight out for dinner before getting a relatively early night. I slept soundly for 9 hours which was excellent. I remember only managing 2 hours of sleep before my first 24 hour race in 2013 but as I have become more and more experienced with big races I have managed to train myself to sleep well the night before the race. There is nothing worse than going into a 24 hour race when you are

5

already tired.

After eating as much as possible at the "all you can eat breakfast" in the hotel's restaurant we headed down to the race village where we met the other two English speaking competitors, Karen Lawrie and Tony Mackintosh from the Isle of Man.

The four of us (Suzanne, Karen, Tony, and I) set up our food tables within the 'International Competitors Tent' and gave Zac our last minute instructions regarding support requirements. Zac was going to be our only support crew until Karen's husband and brother arrived about 10 hours after race start. I can't comment for the others, but I know that Zac did a fantastic job of looking after me during the race - thanks Zac.

Our food table

The course:

Chateau-Thierry is a small town of just 15,000 people located about 50 miles north of Paris, and the 24 hour race-walk is a big annual event for the town.

The race itself starts in the town square and competitors walk 1,300 metres before reaching the course that they will be lapping for the remainder of the 24 hours. At the end/start of each of the 2,400 metre (1.5 mile) laps the walkers go through a local sports hall where they cross the electronic timing mats and see their name and current position/distance on the TV screen before walking through the 'Village des Marcheurs' (race village) where support crew are located in large tents. These large tents provide shelter (for the supporters) when it rains from time to time. This is the only flat section of the course and is probably no more than 400 metres in total.

Inside the sports hall

After leaving the race village we turn left and walk up a short, sharp, steep hill that seems to get steeper and steeper with every lap. But what is worse (at least for me) is that when we reach the top of the hill we then go down a shorter steeper hill that becomes more and more painful as the race goes on. After that we turn right and start the gradual incline up to the top of the course about 1km away.

On the way up to the top of the course we pass the aid station which has a selection of drinks (water, sparking water, orange juice, Coke) as well as a variety of food (fruit, biscuits, chocolate, etc).

When racing in France it would be nice to both speak and understand French but, regardless of what the people at the aid station said to me, all I could say in reply was "Merci" (thank you) which after 20+ hours sounded more like "Mercy"!!!

Shortly after the aid station we reach the top of the course which consists of traffic cones in a circle that we walk around, and a few men in a van noting down our race numbers (to ensure that we have completed the whole lap I assume). Then it is all downhill back to the end of the lap, and through the sports hall, race village, and back up that short, sharp hill again.

This was the first time I had done a race of this length (or any walking race come to think about it) through suburban streets, and it enables you to focus on something other than the race itself as we watched people going about their lives as we walked past their houses every 20 to 30 minutes. At the top of the steep hill that signaled the start of each lap there was a church on one side of the road and a pub on the other side a short distance further on. On Saturday evening people came from everywhere to go to church and it appeared that they were having an outdoor church

The church at the top of the hill

service. The outdoor service seemed to have moved inside on my next lap as the weather wasn't co-operating.

During the night I would see people coming and going from the pub right through to the small hours of the morning when the local baker arrived to open up his bakery. A few laps later and the Church people were back again for Sunday Services.

The race:

For me, it was definitely a race of two halves. I had big goals, and despite finding out on race morning that the course was much hillier than I had expected (I hate hills), I went out at my planned race pace and managed to hold that for about eight hours before starting to slow slightly. I passed through the marathon (26.2 miles) in about 5 ¼ hours and 40 miles in a shade over 8 hours.

Before the start: Suzanne, Me, Karen & Tony

My pace started to drop a little after that as it always does in darkness and I passed 50 miles in 10 hours and 12 minutes. By 12 hours I had slowed to the stage where I knew I was unlikely to achieve my 185km (115 mile) target - 93.3km in 12 hours - but I still felt reasonable and was coming out of my bad patch.

My right shin started to hurt a little while later and it got progressively worse through the early hours of Sunday morning. I was in serious pain every time I lifted my foot off the ground and every time I put my foot back down again. The short, steep downhill section near the start of each lap was probably what precipitated my injury, and after 18 hours I was really struggling to walk down that particular hill. Mentally I was really struggling to keep going. I was feeling very tired (having been awake for about 22 hours already) and another 6 hours of this torture was not a pleasant thought. But I thought I still had a chance of at least achieving a PB and I had put a lot of training into getting this far. I wasn't going to stop now.

The pain got worse, and worse, and worse. Painkillers weren't helping and a few hours later I was finding myself stopping involuntarily every few hundred metres to try and reduce the pain. I remember thinking that a grandmother on a Zimmer Frame would be able to walk faster than me right now!

After a steady, but conservative start that had seen me lapping in 20th/21st place for the first 1 ½ hours before slowly moving up to 10th place at 9 hours, it was disappointing to see that I was now gradually going backwards through the field.

One of the great things about a race like this is that everyone becomes friends. For several hours during the night I had battled against #34, Jeremy Dandoy. At one stage he apologised to me for not being able to speak English. I was too tired to try and apologise for not being able to speak French, but without being able to say more than a word or two to one another, we enjoyed each other's company for what seemed like several hours. In reality it may have been much less than that as in a 24 hour race you start to lose all sense of time. He would get ahead of me occasionally and we would acknowledge each other as we passed in opposite directions at the turnaround at the top of the course, and then I would catch him, we would walk together for a bit, and then I would get ahead of him for a while. It was good fun and a distraction during what was becoming a long race.

As the pain got worse and I started slowing to a speed of less than 5km (3 miles) per hour, walkers whom I had lapped hours earlier were passing me and many of them, regardless of the language they spoke, would try to give me encouragement. Three of those walkers were my English speaking friends, Suzanne, Karen and Tony. Suzanne had been leading the women's race from early on and Tony and Karen had been walking together from the start. I had lapped Suzanne once and Tony and Karen twice, but during the last six hours not only did they all unlap me, but they started to lap me several times over. Whilst I was getting slower and slower, they were all getting faster (or so it seemed to me). They were definitely walking strongly and would finish the race in 9th, 10th and 13th places respectively, with Suzanne taking the overall women's honours and Karen finishing second in the women's race. A superb effort by all three of them.

At 23 hours we were diverted on to a smaller, dead flat, 500 metre lap for the last hour. This was so that we would all be within a short distance of the sports hall when the 24 hour finish siren sounded. I remember arriving at the hall at the end of my last big lap just a few seconds before the 23 hour mark to find about 3 or 4 competitors waiting outside. Not being able to understand what they were saying I continued into the hall and was the first person to be diverted on to the small loop. Immediately I realised that the walkers waiting outside were waiting until they knew it was safe to enter as they, like me, had had enough of the hills on the big lap.

I finally passed the 100 mile mark at 23 hours and 42 minutes and was in so much pain that I wanted to stop then and there. Zac did a great job of talking me into continuing and I hobbled another mile over the next 18 minutes to finish with a total of 162.514km - exactly 101 miles.

This was my worst result from my three 24 hour races - 400 metres less than my first attempt - but I am proud to have completed the full 24 hours. It was definitely my most painful race, but I am hoping that the mental toughness that I needed to get me through the race will help me in future long distance races.

In the end, the race results show that Chateau-Thierry wasn't a course in which I would have achieved my 115 mile target, even if I had had a good race. The race was won by Eddy Roze with an impressive 197.757km, Cedric Varain (193.607km) was second, and Pascal Bunel (who would break the world 6 day record later in the year) was third in 182.901km.

Only nineteen of the fifty starters managed to complete 100 miles or further, and I finished in 18th place. 18th place also happens to be the same placing I got in my last race - the Roubaix 28 hour event last September (when I passed 24 hours with 171.212km - my current PB), and is my worst placing in a race-walking event.

At the finish: Tony, Suzanne, Karen, and me

CHAPTER 4
THAMES PATH 100

Was I tired or did I just have very sore feet?

On the first May bank holiday weekend I competed in the 2015 Thames Path 100 mile ultramarathon (TP100) - a running race from Richmond (near where I live) to Oxford along the Thames Path. And I honestly cannot remember why I slowed down so much over the last 20 miles. They say that you quickly forget the pain of an ultramarathon and only remember the good parts, and that is how you end up entering the next race. You don't remember the pain, the swearing, the absolute exhaustion of the last race, but remember with fondness; the new friends you made, the generosity of the volunteers and organisers who helped you in your hour(s) of need, and the amazing scenery (although this last part doesn't apply to all races - I've done two 100's on a 400 metre track and the scenery in a track race can become a bit repetitive).

Pre-race preparation:

The TP100 was my fifth race of 100 miles or longer and my first trail ultra longer than 40 miles. It was also my first 100 miler without an aid station at least every 2 miles (two of my previous 100's had been on a 400m track and two had been on short road circuits) and the first in which I had had to carry supplies with me.

So the first thing I had to do was 'preparation'. Something I am not overly keen on. I have always preferred to just get stuck in rather than plan anything in any real detail and I don't particularly like to spend money either, so having to buy a compass that I may never need, a map of the Thames Path that I may never need (surely it is just a case of following the river from Richmond to Oxford) and a Goretex jacket that I may never need, as well as a spare head torch and various other things seemed to me to be a bit over the top. Read on and you will find out that it wasn't 'over the top' at all.

I also didn't really put any thought into race-day nutrition. When I did my first 100 miler I went overboard and bought heaps of food for myself and my support crew (my three sons) and then fed myself as I went past the food tent on the far side of the track every 400 metres. And in my next three 100's I took a more relaxed approach to nutrition with a combination of some food that I took with me to the race and some that I picked up as I went past the aid station every lap. I was 5 miles into this race when it suddenly dawned on me that is this event the aid stations were much further apart. The first one was at 11 miles, the second was at 22 miles and the next one was 8 miles further on. There were 13 aid stations in total and maybe I should have been a little more organized than I was!

The first half:

The race start was only a couple of miles from my home so I had the luxury of driving down to race registration, doing the pre-race check-in and then going back home for a second breakfast. I then caught the bus back to Richmond with my wife, Ruth, in time for some pre-race chat with some of the other competitors including Louise Alying, Christian Maleedy and fellow UK Centurion race-walker Mark Haynes. Mark was planning to run the TP100 which meant that I was probably the only person that was planning on walking the whole 100 miles from start to finish.

Shortly before 10am we listened to the pre-race briefing – instructions about how to recognise whether we were on the Thames Path track (sign-posted regularly with acorn symbols), details about the aid stations, reminders about carrying our mandatory equipment and that we would be disqualified if found not to be carrying everything we were supposed to at the random spot checks during the race, etc. And then we were off.

And we're off!

In all my previous 100's I had gone out fast as I was racing for a time, but I had decided before I started that the TP100 was going to be more about walking from Richmond To Oxford and adding a new route to my ever-growing 'Richard Walks London' map than going for a specific time - although it would be nice to keep to my record of never taking longer than 24 hours to walk 100 miles. (See www.richardwalkslondon.com to see where I have walked).

I started at the very back of the field and in the early stages I had company from Catherine Marriott (who unfortunately withdrew at 38 miles) and Welshman, Alan Mann who was using the TP100 as a part of his training towards the Grand to Grand multi-day race in the USA in September.

As I mentioned earlier, I hadn't thought through my nutrition strategy in detail so I had to make some immediate changes (to the nutrition strategy that I hadn't thought through) when I realised that I wouldn't get any food or water until the first aid station at 11 miles (2 hours 20 minutes from memory). My basic plan was to alternate between a sachet of Generation UCan (a sports nutrition supplement) every 2 hours and fruit and biscuits every other hour, but I ended up going through to 11 miles with nothing and then finding that the first aid station didn't have any fruit! They may have had fruit earlier, but I was still in about 255th place out of 265 starters at this stage and they had run out.

Fortunately I love chocolate chip biscuits and every aid station had plenty of these. I started on the UCan at about 3 ½ hours, and this and water was the only liquid I consumed during the whole race. This was the first time that I have gone more than 12 hours in a race without Coke. In fact, possibly the first time in a very, very long time that I have gone more than 12 hours without Coke fullstop!

Apart from getting lost at about 23 miles and losing about 8 minutes as I backtracked to find the correct turnoff, I felt good throughout the first half of the race. I listened to a couple of podcasts and a bit of music, chatted to a few runners and reached the half way checkpoint (actually 51 miles) in Henley after 11 hours and 27 minutes just as it was starting to rain.

By half way I had moved up to 207th place. 35 runners were behind me and 23 had dropped out.

The night section:

Henley was checkpoint number 6 and was the first time that I actually stopped. At each of the previous checkpoints I had been in and out within a minute. On arrival at each checkpoint the fantastic volunteers refilled my bottles whilst I put some biscuits into my pockets and grabbed whatever other food I thought I might like to eat during the next mile or so - often my cupped hands were full with a combination of crisps, chocolate, biscuits, fruit, etc, as I left each checkpoint and I pretty much ate the same thing at each of the 13 checkpoints.

However, on arriving at Henley I stopped for a total of 15 minutes to change into some warmer night clothing (I had only been wearing a long sleeved running shirt up until now), re-apply 2Toms Anti-Blister powder to my feet (which were still in good condition) and also put my head torch on.

I absolutely loved the night section and powered through the course. It took me 5 ½ hours to cover the next 20 miles through to Checkpoint 9 at Streatley and during that time I passed 54 runners! That's one every 6 minutes!

In fact I passed some runners twice because after leaving checkpoint 12 I went the wrong way and ended up in a graveyard at 2am, losing about 12 minutes in total.

I would have got lost many more times throughout the race but whenever I was about to go the wrong way I would hear someone behind me call out, and I did the same a couple times when I saw runners in front of me about to go the wrong way. At one stage I was under a bridge and I asked the runner next to me which way he thought we should go. Before he could answer a "voice from above" called out "up here", and we headed up the stairs onto the bridge that crossed the river.

I arrived at Streatley (71 miles) just before 3am. It wasn't the end of the night section yet, but the results page doesn't have split times again until 91 miles - by which time I will be telling you a different story about the race!

Flying - 71 to 83 miles:

I passed 100km in just under 14 ½ hours, my slowest ever 100km time, but based on how I felt, I was certain that I should be able to still complete the race in under 24 hours. This thought helped drive me through the remainder of the night. According to the results, out of all the runners in the race (182 finished) I was the 86th fastest over the segment between 58 and 71 miles and then, incredibly, my fast walking was faster than all but 46 runners between 71 and 91 miles. I was on fire!

Until 83 miles that is.

The long slow slog to the finish - the last 17 miles:

The sun had come up and I was still feeling good. I caught up with my friend, Louise Ayling, at around 80 to 81 miles and suggested to her that we had a good chance of getting under 24 hours. She was probably struggling a little at this stage and apparently my encouragement spurred her onto an incredible finishing burst for which she later gave me the credit for when I saw her again at the finish. Her last 17 miles were a show of absolute mental willpower and determination that saw her beat me by 53 minutes over the last 17 miles (to save you the maths, that is 3 minutes per mile faster than I would manage).

I don't really know what went wrong. It started to rain a little heavier and that is when I realised why the organisers insisted we carry a Goretex jacket - if I hadn't been able to put that on I suspect I may not have finished. The terrain was not what I would call 'friendly' either. In many places we were walking in long grass and when we weren't on grass it was mud......slippery mud. I was wearing road shoes, with no grip, so you can imagine the difficulty.

I could make lots of excuses, but at the end of the day I just didn't have the mental strength that I expect of myself. Whilst I only lost one place between 91 miles and the finish, after being the 47th fastest between 71 and 91 miles I was only the 133rd fastest over the last 9 miles of the race.

Struggling!

The finish:

It is always a relief to finish a long race. At the end, I had nothing left (physically or mentally) and whilst it had stopped raining and the sun actually came out, I found myself shivering even after a warm shower. I put on all the spare clothing I had and sat in the sun watching the rest of the runners finish, but without really seeing anyone.

Mark and Christian, who I had spoken to before the start, both finished while I was watching (probably) but I didn't see them. I also didn't see Alan (the Welshman) finish either. I called Ruth and she offered to come and collect me rather than me having to catch the train home. That was a real relief because I hadn't really put any thought into the logistics of getting home after the race - other than to take a credit card with me.

My feet hurt like hell. The last few hours on the uneven and muddy ground had caused them to blister badly and they were also swollen (like every other runners feet were). I commented to a few people that I couldn't see how I could possibly line up on the start line at the Grand Union Canal Race (145 miles from Birmingham to London) in three week's time. I was using my blisters as an excuse in the hope that someone would agree with me and I would feel that I could politely withdraw my entry. I can't remember whether anyone did agree with me but I do remember Louise telling me in no uncertain terms that I was definitely not to withdraw from the race!

One final comment:

If you are looking for an adventure, then despite what I might have said in my ramblings above, I absolutely recommend that you enter the Thames Path 100. The volunteers and the organisers did a fantastic job, and it was worth every penny.

I ended up finishing in 25 hours and 2 minutes. My slowest 100 miler to date - almost 3 hours slower than my PB. It was a very tough course, but as the only person in the field of 265 starters that walked every single step, I think I can feel proud to have finished in 113th place out of 182 finishers.

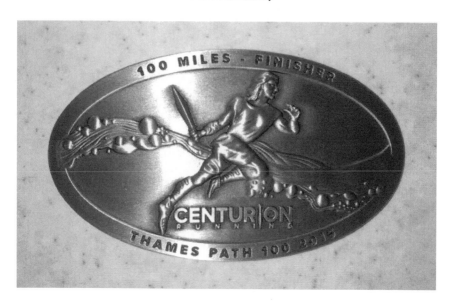

CHAPTER 5
GRAND UNION CANAL RACE

The Grand Union Canal Race is an iconic ultramarathon organised by the legendary Dick Kearn and his legion of volunteers. At just £35 for supported runners and £70 for unsupported (this means that the organisers feed you during the race as well), this is one of the best value for money races in the UK - when calculated on a £££'s per mile basis.

The route follows the Grand Union Canal from the Gas Street basin in Birmingham to Little Venice in London – 145 miles in total. This would be my longest race to date, and once again I was the only walker in a field of 105 starters.

For me, the event started when I finished work at lunchtime on Friday and caught the train from London to Birmingham. The train only takes 1 ½ hours, but it would take a lot longer to walk back – hopefully no longer than 40 hours.

Arriving in Birmingham I checked into my hotel and then went to the local shop to buy some last minute supplies. I had plenty of food in my bag already, but purchased some more - just to be sure.

I also took the time to lay everything out on the bed to check that I had everything I would need for the race - plenty of food (on top of what the organisers would be providing at the checkpoints), a change of shoes (just in case, but in the end unnecessary), three head torches as whilst my two main head torches are extremely bright their batteries only last four hours, and my main nutrition supply for the weekend - 11 sachets of Generation UCan which I poured into 11 bottles with the idea that I would collect one at each checkpoint and "just add water". I also had an assortment of other items including caffeine tablets and painkillers - both of which would come in useful on Saturday night and Sunday. I have often wondered what the hotel cleaner thought when they cleaned my room on Saturday morning - with empty caffeine and painkiller boxes in the rubbish bin as well as some spilt white (UCan) powder on the bathroom cabinet.

Once I had sorted all my race kit and was sure that I hadn't forgotten anything, I headed up to the Travelodge in Broad Street for registration and then to the pub next door to meet some other competitors and have dinner, before an early night. These days I seem to sleep well the night before a race and this was no exception. I was in bed by 9:30pm (the earliest I had been to bed all week) and asleep within minutes. However wasn't long before I woke with cramp in my left calf muscle! I hadn't had cramp when sleeping for a long time. Why tonight?

I lay in bed for a few moments trying to stretch out the cramp, and thinking that my alarm would probably go off shortly. I had had a good sleep and felt ready to get up but on checking my phone I found that it was only 11:30pm!

The next thing I knew it was 4am and the first of three alarms I had set woke me up. My biggest concern before a race is that I won't wake up, so as a backup I also requested a wake-up call from hotel reception for 4:15. If I had waited for that I would still be asleep now as that call never came!

Breakfast would be my last meal sitting down until sometime on Sunday night so I made the most of it - porridge (one of those instant, just add water porridge's that my wife has most mornings but I had never had before), croissants, bananas and some pancakes. Enough to keep me going for the first few hours.

Being an unsupported competitor I was allowed two bags of supplies, which the volunteer crew would ferry from one checkpoint to another, enabling me to just carry the minimum amount that I would need to get me through the few hours between each checkpoint - which were spaced between 10 and 20 miles apart with 10 checkpoints in total.

So I carried my two bags the short walk to the start in Gas Street and then waited patiently talking to some of the other competitors I had met at the pub the previous night and to others with whom I would be sharing the experience that was to come.

Race Start:

Just before 6am we were led down to the canal and Dick gave his final pre-race briefing ("final" because we would be off in a few minutes, but also "final" because after 21 years of organising this iconic race he was handing the reigns over to someone else to take this event forward in the future), and then we were on our way.

I deliberately started right at the back as I was the only walker in the field, so in theory I would be at the back on the field for the first part of the journey. However, as with the Thames Path 100 three weeks ago, there were a few runners who wanted to run slower than I wanted to walk so it wasn't long before I was passing runners. Not that I was walking too fast. I passed the first 5km in about 39 minutes and reached the first checkpoint (10.7 miles) in about 2 hours and 20 minutes.

Down by the canal just before the start

Overall the first section was uneventful other than when I hit my head on the low ceiling as we walked through the first tunnel, and lost my sunglasses into the canal. I just enjoyed walking in new surroundings and taking the occasional photo.

Grand Union Canal shortly after checkpoint 1

Unlike the first four 100 mile (and longer) walking races that I had done, this (and the Thames Path 100 three weeks ago) was a point to point race and as a result there wasn't the opportunity to grab food and drink at the end of every lap like I have become used to. Checkpoint 1 was 10.7 miles into the race, checkpoint 2 at 22.5 miles and checkpoint 3 at 36 miles, and after that the distance between checkpoints ranged from 13 to 20 miles.

These sporadic distances meant that I needed a nutritional strategy. My plan was to collect enough food at each checkpoint to get me through to the next checkpoint as well as one bottle of UCan. At the checkpoints where hot water was available I would also get some porridge or pot noodles - neither of which I had tried in a race before. What I didn't want to do was drink any Coke or consume any high sugar foods. My concern was that once I started on high sugar food/drink I would need to consume more high sugar food and drink at regular intervals throughout the remainder of the race. I didn't want to start down that route too early - especially as I wasn't intending on carrying any Coke between checkpoints until near the end of the race.

One lesson I learnt at the TP100, three weeks earlier, was that I needed a better method of carrying food, so I stashed a number of sandwich sized plastic bags in my food bag and at each aid station I grabbed a plastic bag and filled it with a range of fruit, biscuits, crisps, etc, from the aid station's food table. This worked much better than trying to carry sufficient quantities of food in my hands.

I ate my second porridge of the day (the first one was at breakfast before the start) in the mile or two after leaving checkpoint 3 and it wasn't long before I remembered the first rule of racing – "never try something new on race day". This rule applies to everything to do with your race. Don't try new shoes on race day. Don't wear new clothes on race day (as they could cause chaffing), and DON'T eat food that you haven't had before!

My first bout of diarrhoea hit me at almost exactly 9 hours into the race and for the next six hours I was expelling all the food I had consumed during the day at 20 to 30 minute intervals. Oh the joys of ultra-distance races!

So when I arrived at checkpoint 4 (53 miles) I needed some quick energy and 5 or 6 (small) cups of Coke later I was feeling much better. My intention had been to cover 70 miles, through to checkpoint 5, before darkness and then put on some warmer clothes and my head torch. I was already an hour behind the schedule I had set myself and there was a strong chance that I would need my head torch before we could get to the next checkpoint. So this became my first stop in the race. We were approximately 12 hours in and because of the diarrhoea my pace had slowed dramatically (although I was still passing runners occasionally - I was up to 78th place of 105 starters) and there was a risk that if I didn't put my warmer clothes on now, I would be cold by the time I got to the next checkpoint.

The first night:

I had never suffered diarrhoea in a race before. In fact, my experience was usually the complete opposite. So this was a new experience for me and fortunately, because the race was on a canal trail and it was now getting dark, there were very few people around to witness my frequent stops. There was no need to hide behind a bush or wait until the next public toilet. Just pull over to the side of the trail, do the business, and get going again. Most stops were less than 60 seconds!

Eventually my body returned to normal and I started to enjoy the night time walk along the canal. Dick (the race organiser) had gone to a lot of effort to produce very detailed maps of the race route. Along the canal every single bridge and lock was numbered and the maps told us which bridge to cross and any other details we needed to know. In total there were about 30 bridge crossings and two sections where we moved away from the canal for a mile or so. There were also a few junctions where you needed the map to know whether to go left, right or straight ahead, and Dick's maps were fantastic. There was no chance of getting lost if you followed the maps.

Around 60 odd miles I lost my map and a short while later I saw a runner on the other side of the canal! Fortunately he was going in the same direction as me and at the next lock I crossed the canal to join him, only to find that we were due to cross back to my original side of the canal at the bridge about 100 metres further on. The other runner, whose name I have forgotten, had just started back running again after a short break and was going faster than me. So I borrowed his map for a few moments and noted down the bridge numbers that I would need to cross between where we were and the 70 mile checkpoint, and then let him go. The maps were printed on three double-sided sheets of waterproof A4 paper and whilst we were only on page 1 of sheet 2 I assumed that I would be able to get a replacement map at the next checkpoint so wasn't too concerned.

One of the six maps

I arrived at checkpoint 5 (70 miles) at around 11pm - 17 hours into the race. I was feeling good and found a number of runners at the checkpoint – resting, eating, talking, etc. Many had their buddy runners with them too. From 65 miles you were allowed to have a buddy runner accompany you. This can be good for two reasons - one being safety, as we were into the night section and were running (or in my case, walking) beside a canal. And the other reason is that, as I was finding, it was very easy to lose concentration and slow down without really meaning to. I didn't think I would need a buddy, and to be honest, the way I was feeling I don't know that a buddy would have helped me go any faster anyway, so I hadn't organised one.

My thoughts turned back to the maps and it turned out that there weren't any spare maps available. However one of the runners gave me their map so I could take photos of it on my cell phone, and I also wrote down the bridge crossings - only four bridges to cross during the next 28 miles before we started on the last map sheet at 98 miles.

As soon as I had noted down the bridge crossings I headed off down the canal and into the night again.

I think I may also have had my first Pot Noodles and grabbed some other food supplies at that checkpoint, but there was no need for any more Coke. I was feeling much better.

I enjoy walking at night and I made reasonable progress, arriving at checkpoint 6 (84.5 miles) at around 3am where I had another porridge. I hadn't yet put 2 and 2 together and worked out that it was the porridge that had caused my diarrhoea yesterday.

Sunday:

I was walking along on Sunday morning, 24 hours into the race, and I suddenly realised that a) it was daylight, and b) it was sunny!

It was a cloudy day on Saturday but it looked like it was going to be a hot one today. Guess what? I didn't have any sunglasses.

I arrived at the 100 mile checkpoint just before 8am (26 hours - which incidentally is my slowest of the six 100 milers I have completed) and sat down to change from my warm clothes back into my long sleeved 'Richard Walks London' shirt. One of the volunteers kindly gave me a pair of sunglasses out of his van. I also got my trustee straw hat out of my bag and grabbed some food - another porridge, some UCan, fruit, biscuits, and also a bacon and egg sandwich courtesy of the friendly volunteers at checkpoint 7.

I was 26 hours into the race. It was a beautiful sunny day. I wasn't feeling too tired - thanks to two caffeine tablets every four hours overnight - and I only had 45 miles to go! I had also moved up to 51st place - just inside the top half of the field although I had heard that there had been plenty of DNF's overnight.

My original target had been 36 to 40 hours. 36 hours would have meant an exceptional race and with the benefit of hindsight, knowing that only 28 runners went under 36 hours, was probably a little too ambitious. But with 14 hours to cover the last 45 miles, 40 hours was well within my reach.

But little did I know what a slog the next 45 miles was going to be. Shortly after leaving checkpoint 7 I put 2 and 2 together when I started another two hour period of diarrhoea. Obviously the porridge wasn't such a great idea. It was also daylight now and as well as other competitors on the course there were other people, which meant I had to be a little more discrete during my 5 or 6 toilet stops between 8:30 and 10:30am.

I had also slowed right down, averaging just 5km (3.1 miles) per hour at best. This was also the longest stretch between any of the checkpoints - 20 miles - and it wasn't until 3pm that I arrived at checkpoint 8. It had taken 7 hours to cover just 20 miles!

Am I hallucinating or is that a dinosaur?
30 hours of no sleep and I am seeing things

For the first time in the race runners were passing me. Not that I really cared. I was just focused on moving forward and the hours blurred from one into another. It took me 7 hours to cover 20 miles, but it felt like only 2 or 3. I really had no concept of time.

Checkpoint 8 was the last checkpoint where we would have access to our bags, so even though it was only 3pm I grabbed my head torch because it was likely that it would be dark before we finished. I also knew that I was going so slow that I would get cold very quickly if the weather changed or it got dark, so once again I put my warmer clothes on. Pre-race I hadn't actually thought about the possibility of the race taking me into a second night, and even now it didn't really register with me just how long this race was taking.

Once again I grabbed some food, including my second Pot Noodles, and headed off along the canal. It was like I was on auto-pilot now. A very slow auto-pilot. There was no emotion or feeling. I knew what I had to do and I knew it was probably going to take me at least another 7 hours to do it. Just 25 miles to go.

The rest of the day time section was a blur. I remember buying an ice-cream, being given a slice of pizza by one of the other runners support crew, talking to a couple of runners as they went past me, and then reaching that magic signpost. The one that says "Paddington 13 miles" and points to the left.

Paddington 13 miles!

No more bridge crossings. Just a half marathon to go and all along the same side of the canal. It was 7:30pm and I had been walking for 37 ½ hours. There was just one mile to the last checkpoint. I was in London. Not long to go now.

The second night:

Having read a few other race reports I now know that this section of the canal is dirty and not necessarily the safest of places to walk – especially at night. But I was a zombie now. Since early Sunday morning I had been hallucinating regularly. Everywhere I looked I had been seeing people which then turned out to be trees, rubbish bins, all sorts of objects, but not people. And with two or three hours to go I saw Gollum from Lord Of The Rings swimming in the canal under a bridge.

By this stage I was struggling to walk in a straight line and I am surprised I didn't end up in the canal swimming with Gollum. Regularly I would catch myself as I lurched to the side instead of in the forwards direction that I was aiming for. My legs were so tired that I also found myself stopping on an increasingly regular basis. I would lean against anything that could support me for a quick rest..

The final stretch from checkpoint 10 to the finish was just 12 miles but it took forever. I was down to just over 2 miles an hour (having started on Saturday morning at just under 5 miles an hour) and I was ready to quit. I had never felt this way before. I didn't want to quit because I was in pain. In fact I was long past that pain stage. I was just so tired. I rationalised in my mind that I had done what I set out to do. I had walked from Birmingham to London. I had seen the Grand Union Canal. I didn't need a medal to prove it. All I really needed to do was call my wife and ask her to meet me at that bridge up ahead, and then I could sit in the car and have a sleep.

But for some reason I didn't make that call. I kept plodding along. It was dead calm and there was no one around but me. If I wasn't so exhausted I would have enjoyed the solitude. A couple of runners went past me and I wished them well. There was no way I could 'race' them. I called my wife to say that my expected finish time was now likely to be some time after midnight and I would call her again when I was about an hour from the finish.

And then suddenly I felt good again! For the first time in 15+ hours I felt good! I have no idea what changed, but I was on fire!

I rang my wife to inform her that I was probably less than an hour away from the finish. I was motoring now! At least it felt like I was, but my kilometre split times on my Garmin show that I was still doing less than 3 miles (5km) an hour.

And then just after 1am on Monday morning, having started in Birmingham 43 hours earlier at 6am on Saturday, I finished the 2015 Grand Union Canal Race - official time 43 hours and 1 minute for 54th place.

Some thoughts on the race:

- I had just walked from Birmingham to London!

Birmingham to London via the Grand Union Canal - 145 miles

- I have just walked 145 miles or 233km - my longest ever walk!
- My wife, Ruth, and son, Zac, were fantastic! Not only did they let me spend a whole weekend doing what I love, but they came out at 1am on Monday morning to meet me at the finish line!
- Dick Kearn and his team of volunteers were incredible! Without the support of the volunteers this race would not have been as enjoyable as it was.
- I really don't know why I had such a bad race. Was it too soon

since the Thames Path 100 mile race just three weeks earlier? Was my nutrition plan sub-standard? Or was it just one of those races that don't go to plan?

- I spent 100% of Sunday walking. I also spent 75% of Saturday walking and 4% of Monday. How many people can say that?
- Maybe I should have had a short sleep during the race. If I had slept for 30 minutes at the 100 mile checkpoint, would I have had a better Sunday? The race rules state that you are not allowed to stop for more than 40 minutes at a time or you will be disqualified. I didn't want to take that risk of having a sleep but maybe I should have slept at a checkpoint where someone could have woken me after 30 minutes.
- I can go 43 hours without sleep! In fact, from the time I woke up on Saturday morning until I went to bed on Monday morning was over 47 hours!
- My Garmin said that I burnt 15,600 calories during the race.
- I only had two blisters.
- There were only 63 finishers! That means that 42 starters (1/3rd of the field) didn't complete the race! The Grand Union Canal Race is not as easy as it sounds.
- I am so much tougher mentally now than I was before this race. I am sure that what I went through during the GUCR will help me in my future races
- The finishers medal is the heaviest medal I have ever received

GUCR finishers medal
the start is on one side and the finish is on the other

CHAPTER 6
INJURY AND PHYSIO

Between the Chateau Thierry 24 hour race and the Thames Path 100 miles I only did maintenance training (short, easy training walks), and the same again during the three weeks between the Thames Path 100 and the Grand Union Canal (GUCR). However, after the GUCR I intended to take two weeks of complete rest and then have two or three high mileage weeks before tapering into my next big race – 72 hours in Privas, France.

Unfortunately my right ankle didn't agree with that plan though. The morning after finishing the GUCR I awoke to find it badly swollen and painful to walk on. A week later and it wasn't really much better but I did my weekly parkrun anyway – running rather than walking, which probably wasn't a great idea either. Then after a second week of complete rest I did a parkrun followed by a two hour walk. Dumb idea!

One hour into my walk, I was somewhere in the north London area when my ankle became extremely painful. I didn't have my Oyster (bus) Card or any money with me so had to endure a painful and slow 1 hour walk back to the car.

On Monday I rang my friendly physio who I used to visit regularly as an injured runner. I explained that the reason he hadn't seen me recently was because I had given up running but that I had a sore ankle and could he please take a look at it.

When I saw him the following day he asked what I had done to injure the ankle and I said something along the lines of "I was out walking and afterwards it started to hurt". He asked further questions and I told him that the walk was 145 miles. He asked me to repeat what I had just said as he thought I said I had walked 145 miles! I confirmed that he had heard me correctly the first time.

So for the next 8 weeks I visited the physio twice a week and after a few weeks I was able to start training again. I had to ice my ankle after every walk to reduce the swelling, and only managed one walk of more than two hours.

I find that being injured is like a form of mental torture. It means that I can't do the training that I love to do. For me, training provides the opportunity to explore, to walk in areas that I haven't walked before, and to see sights that many people will never see. I love exploring new paths, trails and roads, and whilst this book is mostly about the races I have competed in during 2015, I have walked considerably further in training than I have in racing, and have many fond memories of the training walks I have done all over London.

So this enforced injury break was extremely frustrating, but the good news is that I went to Privas fully rested ...

CHAPTER 7
PRIVAS 72 HOUR RACE

If you were on holiday in the heat that we had during the Privas 72 hour race you would spend as much time as you could in the water, or in the shade. You would definitely avoid any physical activity and probably wouldn't even go to the beach. It was that hot!

With daytime temperatures of up to 39 degrees and night time temperatures in the 20's, this was definitely the hottest race I have ever competed in.

My initial goals of completing up to 250 miles (400km) during the three day race were unlikely to be met and it would be more a battle of survival than a race - especially during the heat of the day.

Pre-Race:

I left home at 4:30am on Tuesday (the day before the race) to travel to Privas in South, East France. The journey consisted of two bus rides, a short trip on the tube, and then the Eurostar from Kings Cross St Pancras station through to Paris. From there, 2 hours on a French high speed train to Valence TVG, 1 ½ hours on a bus to Privas township, and a ride in a van driven by a Frenchmen named Laurant who didn't speak any English, but I was reasonably confident that he was the guy who had been sent to collect me from the bus stop in the middle of Privas and take me the few miles out of town to the track, and my home for the next four days.

On arriving at the track, I immediately discovered what I was up for. The six day racers were almost 50 hours into their race. No one was running (there were 120 runners and 20 walkers entered) and there were very few people actually on the track - the track being a 1,025 metre circuit comprising mostly of a hard packed cinder and small stone chip surface with a few hundred metres of tarmac.

I met Jamie (Suzanne's son) who informed me that Suzanne was out on the track, but Kathy Crilley (the other English competitor in the six day walking race) was sleeping in the women's changing rooms as it was too hot to sleep in the tents during the day. And Jim, Suzanne's partner and the second member of our support crew, was also sheltering from the heat back at the hotel.

Jim and Jamie had already set up my tent so I decided to take my bag down to the tent and start organising my food, clothes, etc. However, as soon as I opened the tent I realised what Jamie meant about "too hot in the tents" and decided to leave the organising until later on. The heat inside the tent was intense and there was no way I could spend more than a minute inside without becoming soaked in sweat, so I returned to join Jamie in the shade of the big open food tents for an hour or so.

After cheering on Suzanne for a while, Jim, Jamie and I went to McDonalds for dinner. McDonalds is often a pre-race meal for me before ultra-distance events, when I am away from home, as all I am really focused on is consuming as many calories as possible and also ensuring that I am not likely to eat something that might cause stomach upset during the race.

After dinner we watched a bit more of the six day race before walking to Jim and Jamie's hotel where I had an excellent 11 hours sleep - perfect pre-race preparation.

Race start wasn't until 4pm on the Wednesday afternoon, so after a good sleep-in I went to the local supermarket to purchase some more food - a late breakfast, some food for lunch, and some more supplies for the race - and then walked down to the track.

At 2pm we had the pre-race briefing. It was in French but someone, whom I later realised would be the support crew for my biggest competition during the race, offered to act as my personal translator. There wasn't anything surprising in the race briefing, but there was confirmation that toilet facilities must be used at all times - no exceptions. There wasn't really anywhere that an athlete could hide anyway as there were no trees or hedges to use as toilets. There were three sets of toilets - the ones in the men's changing rooms under the grandstand, the ones in the women's changing rooms on the other side of the track, and the unisex public toilets under the back of the grandstand which we would walk past every lap. These were the most accessible as we went right past the doorway every lap, but as a result we also got to smell the aroma coming from the toilets every lap too! And the toilets themselves were squat toilets which were often quite messy - I won't explain further, but just imagine four cubicles being used by 160 athletes who are competing in an ultra-distance race, and what that ultra-distance race can do to your stomach - refer back to my Grand Union Canal Race report if you can't imagine for yourself ☺

The Race Begins:

4pm finally arrives and we are off. There are three competitive walkers in the field (Benedicte Salomez from France, whom I had raced at Roubaix last year and Chateau Thierry this year and beaten both times, and Xabier Salillas from Spain whom I hadn't met before) as well as one other walker and 13 runners. A total field of just 17.

Benedicte, Xabier, and I shared the lead for the first few laps, circling the track in a little over 8 minutes per lap. This was a little slower than I had planned for the early stages of the race, but it was hot so I wasn't going to push the pace. After a while I pulled away from the other two and starting lapping them both as the evening progressed.

I reached 50km in a shade under 7 hours. I had been expecting a time of around 6 ½ hours but given the heat I wasn't concerned about the pace, and as it turned out, this would be my fastest 50km of the race. Due to the heat, I was constantly pouring cups of water over my head to try and keep cool — even during the middle of the night.

Something is wrong:

I like to post updates on facebook during the long races as it gives me something to do other than just focus on walking lap after lap, and I remember posting the words "Something is wrong - going to stop for a sleep" or similar at some stage during the first night of the race. What I am unable to remember is whether that was before my first sleep or between my first and second sleeps.

Early in the race. Walking strong

At around 2:30am, whilst leading the walkers and in third place overall, I suddenly felt absolutely terrible and felt I couldn't go on. I was approaching the end of the track where my tent was located and all I could think about was getting my sleeping bag out and lying down for a few minutes. So I did. I slept for an hour and then resumed the race.

I still didn't feel well though, and whilst I thought at the time that I only did two laps, the lap times on the results sheet show that I walked for an hour before deciding to have another sleep. This time I was off the track for two hours but only slept for one. When I woke up the sun was rising behind the hills and I just couldn't face the idea of getting out of my sleeping bag. So I lay on my camping stretcher beside the track watching the runners and walkers go by and pretending to be asleep.

During the night I had been shivering, even in my sleeping bag with a long sleeved top on in 20+ degree temperatures, and I didn't want to find out what would happen when I stood up and started walking. So I didn't.

Thursday:

I finally started walking again around 6:45am, and other than a few breaks for some shade, I trudged around the track the best I could for eight hours until the heat told me I needed to shelter for a while. An afternoon rest in the shade at the top of the grandstand seemed like a good idea and I carried my camping stretcher up there, took my shoes and top off, and went to sleep in the shade for 1 3/4 hours.

By the time I woke up and resumed the race I was third walker, 20+km behind Benedicte, and 11th overall in the field of 17. The race was not going to plan! I walked a few laps at 8:30/lap pace and felt good. It was still hot, but I told myself that when the sun went down tonight I was going to start racing again.

After about an hour I took a short break for dinner - the race organisers supplied a sit-down breakfast and dinner each day which athletes could partake in if they desired - and then started my push through to my 48 hour goal/target - the New Zealand 48 hour record.

New Zealand 48 hour race-walking record:

In the first 24 hours I had covered just 110km. The existing NZ

48 hour record (the easiest record in the NZ ultra-distance record book) was just 230.25km. I had already beaten that when I walked 233km in 43 hours in the Grand Union Canal Race back in May, but that wasn't a walking race with walking judges, so it didn't count.

My intention before the race was to cover 280km, or more, in the first 48 hours of the race and then hopefully get through to at least 400km (250 miles) by the finish, but the high temperatures had put paid to that idea before the race even started. 120km in the second 24 hour period was still possible though, and when I resumed walking after dinner I had 20 hours in which to cover about 110km - I can't remember the exact numbers unfortunately, but I knew it was still possible.

Disaster struck shortly after 10pm when a blister burst on my left heel and I was slowed to a limp through to the end of the lap and a visit to the medical tent. I expected it would be a relatively short stop to get the heel taped up, but when the doctor saw the state of my toes he insisted on draining and taping the four blisters on the front of my foot as well as dealing with the blister on my heel, and I ended up spending exactly an hour in the medical tent. I refused to show him my right foot though as I feared that might be just as bad. The track surface had badly cut up and blistered both feet, but I had to get moving and I promised to bring my right foot back to see him after 4pm tomorrow.

I left the medical tent with about 16 hours to go (until 48 hours would be up) and, from memory, about 90km to cover to get the record. For the next 16 hours all I did was try and remember my time at the end of each lap so that I could calculate how long the current lap took me when I saw the clock again. I had to complete each lap in under 11 minutes average time, including any breaks I might need during the next 16 hours. That might sounds easy (17 minute per mile pace), but add the heat into the equation and I promise you, it was definitely not easy. Sometimes I would get to the end of the lap and forget what the time was at the start of the lap, so I would have to hope it was a good time and get on with the next lap.

About once an hour I would take a few seconds to stop and read the scoreboard TV screen which was off to one side of the track and couldn't be viewed without stopping. It showed the position of each athlete and their total distance, but it wasn't always 100% up to date. I remember watching it once when my distance suddenly increased by two laps while I was watching the scoreboard. So whilst it showed me gradually moving up the field, I could never be 100% sure how many laps I had done or how many I had to go.

I stopped for a short rest and celebratory can of Coke upon passing both 100 miles (35 ½ hours) and 200km (42 hours I think) but other than that it was 16 hours of relentless forward momentum, watching the clock and trying to calculate my lap times and what pace I needed to maintain to get that record.

With an hour to go I was getting concerned that I wouldn't make it. I tried messaging Ruth figuring that she could follow the results online and let me know whether I was going to make it, but she wasn't home. I stopped at the scoreboard again and calculated that I should complete the lap that would see me completing 231km with about 15 minutes to spare. This would give me time to do one more lap before the 48 hours was up so that I could at least raise the record distance to 232km. I don't know why that seemed better to me than 231km, but it did.

The race announcer was aware that I was close to breaking the NZ record and made a few announcements to the supporters and other athletes (if any of them were listening) in French. Just a little bit more pressure. I had to make sure I did it now.

Finally, at roughly 3:53pm, 47 hours and 53 minutes after starting the race, I completed the lap that I thought would take me through to 232km and announced that that was far enough, I wasn't going to add a part-lap to the record distance. I had beaten the NZ record!!

A few minutes later I found out that I had actually walked one lap further than I thought I had. The new NZ 48 hour race-walking record was now 233.075km! I had beaten the old record by 2.7km.

It had taken a lot out of me though, both physically and mentally. There was no way I could continue immediately, even if I wanted to. It had been almost 24 hours since I woke from my last sleep and I intended to have a bit of R&R before continuing.

I headed to the medical tent first, but when they saw my feet and I explained that my intentions were to take a bit of a break, the medical staff asked me to have a shower first so as to reduce the risk of infection when they tended to the blisters, and to enable them to see the blisters. My feet were black from the dust and dirt on the track so I walked back to my tent and picked up my towel and a change of clothes and then spent the next 30 minutes, or more, carefully removing the tape that the medical staff had so expertly applied to my left foot the previous night.

After a shower I spent an hour or more in the medical tent getting numerous blisters on the top, bottom, and sides of both feet drained and taped so that I would be able to continue walking. I had dinner and then a 1 ½ hour sleep. In Total, I had 7 ½ hours R&R. Talk about luxury. My wife commented after the race that I went to France for a holiday and did a bit of walking while I was there, and when I look at the amount of time I had off the track I can see why she thinks that.

48 hour record completed. And the medical tent behind me awaits

The Final Day:

When I stopped at 48 hours I was leading the walking section, 26km ahead of Benedicte and 32km ahead of Xabier, and I was third overall, just 1km behind the second placed runner, but 7 hours later I had once again slipped down the field in both categories and was 7th overall and second walker behind Benedicte.

It was close to midnight when I decided to start walking again. There were 16 hours to go until the race finish and I was thinking that maybe I could complete another 87km to get to 320km (200 miles). That would be a good result given the conditions. If I couldn't get to 320km then 300km should be easily achievable.

I walked through the night, and didn't stop for breakfast as I wanted to get as far as I could before the day started to heat up. I passed Benedicte again during the night. I think she took a few breaks and I remember her telling me at one stage that she was suffering. But as the day started to warm up I started to struggle again and Benedicte slowly unlapped herself to the stage where we were both on the same lap - a lap that took me 24 minutes to complete!!

I was dead on my feet. I had given the race everything mentally and, I thought, physically, and I had no more to give. This was the hardest event I had ever competed in. I had given up on the 320km target long ago and now it looked like I wouldn't make 300km either.

I decided that was it. I had completed 67 hours of a 72 hour race, but I couldn't do any more. I had done 280km - 47km further than I had ever walked before.

Suzanne was at the food tent when I completed the lap and told her of my plan - which was to watch the rest of the race from the shade in the grandstand. I picked up some food and an empty water bottle and Suzanne ensured that I made it around the half lap to the grandstand safely. I used the cold water tap at the grandstand to fill my bottle and then lay down on one of the grandstand concrete steps to rest. After a while I fell asleep - only for 45 minutes because I wasn't really that tired. I was just totally stuffed (to put it politely). After about four hours of resting I decided to take some photos of the athletes and slowly walked around the track taking photos until I found both Kathy and Suzanne at the food tent.

There was now only 30 minutes until the finish so we decided to walk another couple laps and just enjoy the last stages of what had been a difficult few days for us all - Suzanne had been off the track for two days due to illness and both Kathy and I had struggled with the heat.

At 72 hours for me, and 144 hours for Suzanne and Kathy, the final gun sounded and we all stopped and put our small numbered piece of wood, which we had been given a lap earlier, on the ground so that actual distances could be measured.

For me the total distance was 283.6km. Kathy managed 344.1km which is a UK age group record for the six day event, and Suzanne completed 414.8km.

In the 72 hour race I finished second walker, 18km behind Benedicte, and 7th overall.

Finished!!

In addition to completing my longest ever walk, I had also raised just over £1,000 for the Make-A-Wish Foundation by promoting my walk through Just Giving's website. I am aiming to raise more money for charity in future walks and £1,000 from my first fundraising attempt was a great start.

Fitbit Analysis:

I wore my Fitbit during the race and it is thanks to this that I know so much about how much rest I had. My original reason for wearing the Fitbit was that I thought it would be interesting to know how many steps I covered in a 72 hour period (350,600), and I would also be able to see whether my cadence (the number of steps per minute) changed much during the race. Also, Fitbit measures how much sleep you have - which was a total of six hours in five separate sleeps ranging from 45 minutes to 1 3/4 hours in duration.

My average cadence during training is around 700 to 750 steps every five minutes - or 140 to 150 steps per minute. When I am doing speedwork my cadence will increase to around 180 steps per minute, but most of my training consists of walks ranging from 10 to 30 miles in distance at 140 to 150 cadence.

It was interesting to see that other than the last day and the section during the heat of the day on Thursday, my cadence was consistently around 600 to 650 steps every five minutes (120-130 steps per minute). Once I resumed walking at around 55 hours into the race, after a 7 hour break, I never actually got my cadence back up to the levels it had been earlier in the race. Was this due to mental or physical fatigue, or both? Or was it because my 7 hour break was too long and I just couldn't get back into it? I'm not sure.

The Fitbit analysis also showed how much rest I had. It told me that out of 72 hours I had six breaks of an hour or more and that those six breaks added up to over 19 hours of rest! Add in the smaller breaks and I only barely managed to spend 50 hours actually walking!

Again, as my wife said, I went to France for a holiday and did a bit of walking while I was there ☺

Lessons Learned:

This was my first multi-day race. I had done the Grand Union Canal Race in 43 hours, but that was without sleep and didn't quite take up two full days. This race took three complete days.

It didn't go to plan, but it taught me a lot that will help me in future races. Some of the lessons learned include:

- Be more organised.
  Some of the European athletes were extremely well organised. Before Privas, I had done two other ultra-distance races in France and you often see microwave ovens, fridges, etc, in some of the athlete's tents. And if not, they often have all their supplies organised into different containers - i.e. fruit, biscuits, sports nutrition, etc, separated from first aid supplies, spare socks, sun block, and other equipment. Something I can definitely improve on and especially important if self-supported as you want to be able to quickly access what you need when you need it.
- Big walk-in tent.
  A bigger walk-in sized tent would also have been much better than having to get on my hands and knees when looking for what I needed from the tent.
- Proactive feeding.
  Don't get me wrong, Jim and Jamie provided great support, but we didn't have a proactive feeding plan and as a result I had heaps of food left over at the end which I had completely forgotten about during the race. I had eaten a lot at the official food tent, but I had purchased plenty of food for the race which I didn't touch - including Pot Noodles (500 calories per cup) and jelly (100 calories per cup). I also suspect that I didn't eat enough calories on a regular enough basis. I often went several laps without food. At a minimum, next time I will set my watch alarm to remind me to eat regularly, but better still, ensure that my support team put some food into my hands as I go past them every lap (or two at most) without me needing to ask or think about it.
- I can't think for myself.
  When I have been walking for x hours I am not going to be thinking straight, and therefore may make bad decisions. The decision to have a 7+ hour break after completing 48 hours was wrong. The decision to stop after 67 hours was wrong. I probably made other wrong decisions too. In my next multi-day race I need someone to make decisions like this for me. Someone to tell me when to sleep, when to eat, etc. I should be walking

only and leave everything else to someone else. What I need is a 'handler' - someone who does everything for me other than the actual walking.

- Shoe modification.

I took 3 pairs of shoes to Privas and wore each pair at different stages of the race - the first time I have changed shoes during a race. One of the pairs was an extra size bigger than my normal shoes to accommodate my feet if they swelled (which they did). What I didn't expect was the blisters. Both feet blistered badly around the area of the little toe. Talking to some more experienced athletes after the race, several suggested that I should have cut out the side of my shoe to make more room for my toes. This was an option I was aware of but didn't think to try during the race.

- Tape toes before the start.

The medical experts did an excellent job with taping my feet. I used 2Toms Anti-Blister powder which I applied to my feet several times but in a multi-day race I think that taping is probably a better option.

- Remove negative thinking.

This is the third time that I have allowed negative thinking to get to me, and the third time that I have failed as a result. In Roubaix last year I was targeting 200km in 28 hours, and when I realised that that goal was unlikely with about three hours to go, I was suddenly so tired that I needed a sleep before I could continue - and I finished with 186km losing four places in the last four hours. Then in the Thames Path 100 in May, at around 83 miles I realised that I would be unlikely to finish within 24 hours. I was with Louise Ayling at the time and she had the opposite, positive, view. Her finishing time ended up being an hour faster than mine! And this time, I think it was when I, probably mistakenly, realised that I wouldn't make 300km that I gave up at 67 hours. Had I continued rather than taking a 4 ½ hour break, who knows what might have happened.

- Train to walk slowly.

Most of my training is at an average speed of about 5 miles (8km) per hour with occasional faster walks or faster segments within my training walks. But even in a 24 hour race I don't walk that fast. So should I be training at a slower pace? I don't know. But I do think that I need to do more 24 hour races as training for the longer, multi-day races so that I can get my body used to sleep deprivation and walking at a slower pace when already exhausted. Perhaps I need to do less everyday training and more ultra-distance racing - with some races simply being training for other races.

- Multiple goals may not be a good idea.
  I had a goal to break the NZ 48 hour record as an interim goal, but in reality that was probably more important to me than the goal for the whole race. And therefore, mentally, once I reached that 48 hour goal my race was pretty much over and it was very difficult to keep myself going through to the finish - as we saw.

I don't mean my reflection to sound negative with the above list, but at the end of the day the only failure is the failure to learn from your experiences and I think I have learnt some lessons that will help me greatly in my future races.

These feet have just carried me 283km in 72 hours!

CHAPTER 8
A TRIP TO NEW ZEALAND & A MARATHON PB

The 72 hour race finished on Saturday afternoon, and on Sunday I travelled back to London by bus and train – a 12 hour journey. I then put my feet up for 1 ½ days before a 32 hour flight to New Zealand to see family and friends.

In my second weekend in New Zealand, and on next to no training other than a couple of gentle walks during the previous week, I competed in a local marathon. The 5 Bridges Marathon in Lower Hutt is one of the few marathons that I am aware of that not only has a separate walkers division, but a separate start time for walkers (one hour before the runners start) and, as I felt as though I had already recovered from Privas, I thought I would see whether all the training I had done over the last 9 months would help me achieve a good marathon time. My previous best marathon time was 4 hours and 53 minutes from the same race in 2013 and I felt that I could beat that assuming that I didn't die a horrible death because my body hadn't really recovered.

As it happened, I led from start to finish and took 1 ½ minutes off my best time, finishing in 4:51:58 - Beating my own course record in the process.

I took another week and a half off after the marathon to recover and return to the UK, and then I started training towards my last race of the year – the Roubaix 28 hour race and an attempt at the NZ 200km record.

CHAPTER 9
ROUBAIX 28 HOUR RACE

The Roubaix 28 hour race was first held in 1954 and has been held every year since, making it one of the oldest continuously run race-walking races in the world.

When I competed last year this was my longest race to date and only my third race of 100 miles or longer. Going into this year's event I had completed four races of 100 miles, or longer, in the previous 6 months and was in excellent condition, both mentally and physically. My goal was to complete at least 200km and ideally a little further than that as the current New Zealand 200km race-walking record was 27 hours and 40 minutes. It would be the perfect ending to my racing year if I could beat that time.

As with last year, there were only two English speaking walkers in the race. Suzanne Beardsmore, who was coming off the 6 day race at Privas in August, and myself. We were being supported by Suzanne's partner Jim and fellow centurion race-walker, Sarah Lightman. There were also two teams of GB walkers competing in the 24 hour relay event which accompanied the main race.

Jim, Sarah, Suzanne and I traveled to Roubaix by car on Friday, the day before the race. After arriving in Roubaix we went straight to the track to set up our tent (to be used by Jim and Sarah as shelter during the race before checking in to our hotel and joining many of the other individual and relay competitors for dinner at a local restaurant on Friday evening. One of the things I love about the French ultra-distance race-walking circuit is that at every race you make new friends and meet old friends again. The competitors come from all over Europe and speak many different languages. As a result, you often find yourself communicating in very basic English, French, or maybe even in sign language. This year was no exception, with walkers coming from New Zealand (me), England, France, Holland, Russia, Germany, Belgium, and several other European countries.

Race Day:

On Saturday morning we visited a supermarket to purchase some last minute food supplies and then set up the rest of our equipment trackside to ensure that Jim and Sarah would be able to provide the best possible support. A job that they did perfectly.

The race itself started in the town square in Roubaix at 11am so we left Sarah at the track and traveled the short distance into Roubaix with Bernard Six, a local resident who has been supporting the English race participants for as many years as anyone can remember. It was a beautiful sunny morning driving from the track to the town centre, a big improvement over the wet weather from Friday, but no sooner had we arrived at the race start and the heavens opened with a torrential downpour that lasted about ten minutes. During this time we sought refuge in a local cafe, had a drink and made use of their toilet to relieve pre-race nerves. Fortunately, once the rain stopped we didn't have any weather problems again - until we arrived back in England on Monday afternoon!

Tour of Roubaix:

The first 18.5km was a tour of Roubaix which is a fun way to start the race. We started outside the town hall and, in my case, followed the leaders through the often narrow streets of the town. My aim for this stage of the race was to keep the pace at between 7:30 and 7:45 per kilometre (12 to 12 ½ minutes per mile) and whenever my pace increased above this speed I would deliberately slow down and let myself drift slowly back through the field, being careful not to allow the gap between myself and the walker in front to become too big as I may need to rely on them for directions. There was only one time that I went around a corner to find the street in front of me empty, but fortunately most corners were well marked with green arrows so I didn't have any problems and didn't get lost along the route.

Navigating the streets of Roubaix

I arrived at the Parc Des Sports, where we would be racing over a 1.982km circuit for the remainder of the event, 2 hours and 23 minutes into the race and in 31st place, and then I started to race!

Around and Around:

For me this was probably the most uneventful race of this distance that I have ever done. I'm not complaining; the opposite actually. The race went perfectly. I didn't have any really low points during the race or any real problems. I simply walked around the circuit lap after lap after lap. At the end of each lap I would pass the electronic timer and then see my name on the TV together with my cumulative distance and current position in the field, and as the distance grew, the position slowly came down. There was never a time when my position went up; meaning that throughout the race I was passing people which gave me huge motivation. Just past the TV screen either Jim and/or Sarah would be waiting to feed and/or water me. It was a 25 ½ hour eating and walking festival. There was also an aid station approximately half way around the circuit where I would often grab another drink or a banana as I walked past.

Unlike recent races where I have tried to remain sugar free for as long as possible (and in the Thames Path 100 I completed the whole 100 miles without any sugary food or drink at all) I had decided that I would fuel myself mainly on Coke, fruit and biscuits along with ham and crisps, and at least every second lap (every 4km) Jim or Sarah would hand me something to eat. I was in paradise; having a great race and something to eat at least every half hour. What more could I ask for?

My lap times were extremely consistent too. Averaging around 15:30 to 16:00 per lap in the early stages and then slowing a little once it was dark, but with a fastest lap of 14:48 and a slowest lap of 18:08 (I stopped for a quick toilet break) I can't complain, and most of the 94 laps I completed were in the 15 to 17 minute range.

The circuit consisted of about 300 metres on a compacted cinder track which could have been very messy if it had rained throughout the race, but turned out to be a great surface other than the occasional small stone that would bounce up into my shoe. I had to stop three times during the race to remove stones from my shoes but this wasn't a major issue. The rest of the circuit consisted of three separate out and back sections on a tarmac surface, with one being dead flat and the other two being slightly uphill - but only with a few metres of elevation change so nothing much to worry about.

I found myself getting into a rhythm and the laps flew by. With the three out and back sections we got to see the other athletes throughout the race which was fantastic. Occasionally I would use the opportunity to calculate how many minutes or seconds I was behind someone and then check again on the next out and back section to see whether I was closing the gap. This became especially useful and motivating during the last few hours of the race.

I passed 100km shortly after midnight in a time of 13 hours and 18 minutes. Not my fastest time for 100km in a race of this distance but something I was completely comfortable with. My aim had been to complete the first 100km in 13 hours flat but I was happy with 13:18.

I arrived at 100 miles in a 28 minute PB of 21 hours and 45 minutes, and was still going strongly, and still moving up through the field. From memory I was in about 14th place at this stage.

I wanted to achieve a decent distance over 24 hours too as I wanted to qualify for the prestigious Paris-Alsace race which is held each June with entry being by invitation only. Last year my best distance for 24 hours was 172km and the cut-off for invitations appeared to be 173km, so I wanted to beat that distance. I didn't actually intend to do Paris-Alsace next year though. It is an extremely brutal race held over 5 days on the roads of France with at least one stage being very mountainess (and I don't enjoy hills as we found out at Chateau Thierry earlier this year) and not something that I want to do until I am a little more experienced. But at the same time I wanted to prove to myself that I could qualify if I wanted to do the race. I managed to complete 176.6km in 24 hours by which stage I was in 10th position overall, and immediately after the race the Paris-Alsace organiser invited both myself and Suzanne to compete next year. Suzanne has accepted, but I have declined the invitation.

200km New Zealand Race-Walking Record:

Next on the agenda was to get through to 200km in less than 27 hours and 40 minutes. Having passed 100 miles in 21:45 I had almost six hours to complete less than 40km and thought that would be a breeze. But for some reason I slowed a little in the next 10km and by 24 hours I knew I still had to concentrate on the job at hand if I was to achieve my goal.

With the circuit being a 1.982km lap which we had started after already walking 18.5km, the 200km mark was not at the end of a lap and I was actually going to have to cover 200.9km in order to get an official time for 200km. At the speed I was walking, 900 metres equated to about 7 minutes so I actually had 3 hours and 40 minutes to cover 24.3km. Easy to achieve at the start of the race, but I had already been walking for 24 hours!

This is where Sarah comes into the story big time. I don't remember exactly when, but at around 24 hours Sarah started pacing Suzanne for a while as Suzanne was struggling. They did 12km together in total so I guess it must have been sometime after 25 ½ hours into the race that Sarah then started to pace me. Initially she would walk with me for one lap, let me walk a lap alone, and then walk with me for another lap. The company was great and my pace picked up just enough to give me confidence that I could get the record.

Sarah pacing me

Jim continued to feed me regularly too and it got to the stage where I was eating every lap as well as drinking Coke at the aid station on the other side of the circuit. Things were going really well. I moved into 8th place on the 200km lap and completed that lap (200.9km) in a new New Zealand 200km record time of 27 hours, 27 minutes, and 12 seconds!

No Time For Celebration:

The problem was that two laps before reaching 200km we worked out that the guy in 7th place was only six minutes in front of me, and on the same out and back section during the 200km lap he was only three minutes in front of me. We also worked out that it was possible for me to complete another two full laps after finishing the 200km lap; meaning that there was a very strong chance that I could move into 7th place before the end of the race if I kept pushing it. So no time for celebration other than to grab a can of Coke from Jim and keep on walking.

It turned out to be an anti-climax though as half way around the penultimate lap I had almost caught 7th place when he stopped at the toilets! He must have been desperate to stop with less than 25 minutes still to race.

I had built up momentum and kept the pace going right through to the finish with two of my fastest laps of the race.

In the end I completed a total of 205.090km in the 28 hours and finished in 7th place. By far the best ultra-distance race performance of my life.

Some Analysis:

Firstly, I wore my Fitbit during the race and was surprised after I finished to find that in each 14 hour half I had walked an almost identical number of steps - 112,500 steps in the first half and only 500 less steps in the second half.

Looking at my lap splits I walked almost exactly 105km in the first 14 hours and 100km in the second.

Only 500 less steps but 5,000 metres less distance.

It's over! And these feet have just carried me 205km!

When I calculate my average stride length, less than 500 metres of the 5km slowdown in the second half was due to the reduced number of steps. The remaining 4.5km slowdown was due to a 4 centimetre reduction in average stride length!

If I had maintained the same stride length throughout the whole race I could have walked almost 210km.

Next, my lap splits. Once we were onto the circuit I completed 94 laps in 25 hours and 34 minutes. An average lap time of 16:19.

My fastest lap was 14:48 which I did twice (laps 4 and 5) and my slowest was one of my toilet stop laps - lap 74 which took 18:08.

30 laps took between 15:00 and 15:59 and 44 laps took between 16:00 and 16:59.

52 laps were slower than my 16:19 average and 42 were faster.

My 68th and 69th laps were my 7th and 5th fastest. This is because I was lapped by the race leader, Dmitriy Osipov from Russia, just after 151km and decided to sit on his shoulder for a couple laps - I lasted 2 ½ laps before deciding to ease the pace a little.

And outside of laps 69 and 70, my last two laps (laps 93 and 94) were my fastest since lap 24, almost 20 hours earlier!

Lastly, I covered more distance in the last four hours than everyone but one person - 28.4km!

Also, I didn't sit down once during the whole race. 28 hours on my feet!

Injinji Toe socks:

In all my races and long training walks this year I have been coating my feet in 2Toms Anti-Blister powder with great success. I have had very few blisters compared to usual, other than the Privas 72 hour race where my feet were badly damaged by blisters. So for Roubaix I decided to use both 2Toms Anti-Blister powder and Injinji toe socks.

The result: one very small blister on the small toe of my left foot (one of the three toes that lost toenails at Privas) and some blistering on the sides of both heels. Also a small hole on the big toe of my left foot (the big toe of the sock, not my foot).

I was wearing the Injinji Performance Liner sock which is much thinner than the normal Injinji socks and I think the idea is to wear another thin pair of socks over the top which is something I will do next time as I think that would prevent the heel blisters.

Overall I was happy with the result and will definitely use the combination of 2Toms Anti-Blister Powder and Injinji Socks again.

Thanks Jim and Sarah:

Lastly, I want to thank Jim and Sarah once again for their fantastic work in supporting both Suzanne (who finished 3rd female with a distance of 185.629km) and I. Obviously it is your job to support Suzanne, Jim - given that you live together - but I wouldn't have achieved the distances and times I did without the support and encouragement you both gave me during the race. Thanks.

And Sarah, I look forward to reciprocating when you race Roubaix next year ☺

Jim, Sarah, and Suzanne

CHAPTER 10
WHAT NEXT?

Firstly, thanks for reading this book. Hopefully you might have got something out of reading about my year of ultra-distance race-walking. I mean more than just helping you get to sleep at night.

2016 is going to be another big year for me. I have got five races of 100 miles or more planned plus the possibility of a 165 mile training walk to raise money for charity.

At the time of writing this book, it is two months since Roubaix and I am currently taking time out to recover from a few minor injury problems. Nothing too serious, but I have put my body through a lot in 2015 and it needs a break.

At this stage the plan is to take things easy through until the end of the year and then start training again in January. However, rather than doing high mileage over the winter I want to slowly ease back into it and slowly build up the mileage while also working on technique.

I hope to do the Bourges 24 hour race in France in late February as a long training walk, and may follow that up in March with the 165 mile training walk for charity. After that I have both the Dutch Centurions 100 mile race and the Grand Union Canal Race in May, two weeks apart. This will be hard. This year I had three weeks rest between the Thames Path 100 and the GUCR, and struggled in the latter. A two week break between two 100+ mile races will not be easy, but will be good training for later in the year.

And then in August I will do my first big race of the year – an attempt to go under 21 hours for 100 miles at the UK Centurions race in August. All the other races will be training towards both this and my biggest race ever – the 6 jours de France (Privas 6 day race). Yes, I am going back for more punishment - double the punishment in fact. But the good news is that the race organisers have moved the 2016 edition of the race to October rather than August which hopefully means the weather will be much cooler.

All these races take a lot of training and also cost money for travel and various expenses. So thank you for purchasing this book. In a small way you have contributed to help me complete these races in 2016.

Lastly, if you would like to follow my progress in 2016, you will find me on Facebook (www.facebook.com/richardwalkslondon) and Twitter (www.twitter.com/richwalkslondon).

I also have a blog (RichardWalksLondon.com) and on the blog I have an 'equipment' page with links to some of the equipment I have mentioned in this book. If you want to purchase anything I have mentioned in this book, please click on the link from my equipment page (http://www.richardwalkslondon.com/equipment) as in some cases I earn a small commission from the likes of Amazon when anyone clicks on my link, and that all helps towards funding my next race.

Thanks for your support,

Richard McChesney
Ultra-Distance Race-Walker